The Grace Gift

The Gospel is all about God's grace through Jesus Christ.
That's why Paul calls it "the gospel of the grace of God"
(Acts 20:24) and "the word of his grace" (Acts 14:3)

The Grace G.I.F.T
© 2020 Crystalyn Mason

Published by Living Water Book,
Christian Division of Butterfly Typeface Publishing House,
Little Rock, Arkansas 72201
ISBN 978-1-7357073-6-5

All rights reserved. This book is protected by the copyright laws of the United States of America. This book may not be copied or reprinted for commercial gain or profit. Any portion thereof may not be reproduced or used in any manner whatsoever without the express written permission of Crystalyn Mason except for the use of brief quotations in a book review or occasional page copying for personal or group study is also allowed and encouraged.

Unless otherwise indicated, scripture quotations are taken from The New King James Version Bible and The Common English Bible.

Scripture quotations identified NKJV are from The New King James Version® Copyright© 1982 by Thomas Nelson, Inc used by permission all right reserved.

Scripture quotations identified CEB are from The Common English Bible Copyright ©2011 used by permission All rights reserved.

Please note that Living Water Books of Butterfly Typeface Publishing House capitalizes specific pronouns to scripture that refers to the Father, Son, and Holy Spirit and may differ from some publisher's styles.

John 7:38
He who believes in me, as the scripture has said,
Out of his heart will flow rivers of living water.

The Grace Gift

God's Image For Transformation

CRYSTALYN MASON

DEDICATION

This book is dedicated to my Lord Adonai and my husband. I honor you for the unconditional love and support that you have given me on this journey. Honey-Love, you are my strength in the midst of my weaknesses. Your faithfulness on this journey with me represents how Elohim Immanuel never leaves or forsakes us. Your representation of God's character allows me to experience God's grace, healing, and deliverance. The love of Christ is transforming me through you. Thank you, Jesus, for my husband and our transparent relationship.

FOREWORD

As a pastor, you always want to see people grow in Christ, and that is precisely what I've witnessed in the life of this inspiring young woman of God. I have had the privilege of being her and her family's pastor for many years, and I have no doubt of who she is in Christ.

Her life has exemplified one who has the heart to see others experience the full joy of living under the shadow of the Most High. She is definitely living proof, "If you are faithful to God, God will be faithful to you." I believe you'll find that this book was written with that heart at the forefront of every word. I know it will draw you closer to the Lord.

In HIS Service,
Rev. Bud Womack, Lead Pastor

THE GIFT OF LOVE

The image of Christ within us should burn bright so others can see and desire Go. We are a city on a hill sent to shine the light of Jesus into souls.

1 John 4:19
We love because he first loved us.

Grace is the basis of who we are

·Our Christian identity:
"By the grace of God, I am what I am, and his grace toward me was not in vain." (1 Corinthians 15:10 ESV)

·Our standing before God:
"Through Him, we have also obtained access by faith into this grace in which we stand, and we rejoice in hope of the glory of God." (Romans 5:2)

·Our behavior:
"For our boast is this, the testimony of our conscience, that we behaved in the world with simplicity and godly sincerity, not by earthly wisdom but by the grace of God, and supremely so toward you." (2 Corinthians 1:12)

·Our living:
For if, because of one man's trespass, death reigned through that one man, much more will those who receive the abundance of grace and the free gift of righteousness reign in life through the one man Jesus Christ."(Romans 5:17). Likewise, husbands, live with your wives in an understanding way, showing honor to the woman as the weaker vessel, since they are heirs with you of the "grace of life," so that your prayers may not be hindered.
(1 Peter 3:7)

·Our holiness

For God saved us and called us to live a holy life. He did this not because we deserved I, but because that was his plan from the beginning of time to show us his grace through Christ Jesus." (2 Timothy 1:9)

·Our strength for living

"You then, my son, be strong in the grace that is in Christ Jesus," (2 Timothy 2:1 NLT) Do not be led away by diverse and strange teachings, for "it is good for the heart to be strengthened by grace, not by foods, which have not benefited those devoted to them.
(Hebrews 13:9)

·Our Way Of Speaking

"Let your speech always be gracious." (Colossians 4:6)

·Our Serving

"As each has received a gift, use it to serve one another, as good stewards of God's varied grace." (1 Peter 4:10)

·Our Sufficiency

"My grace is sufficient for you." (2 Corinthians 12:9) "God is able to make all grace abound to you so that having all sufficiency in all things at all times, you may abound in every good work." (2 Corinthians 9:8)

·Our Participation In God's Mission

When he came and saw the grace of God, he was glad, and he exhorted them all to remain faithful to the Lord with steadfast purpose (Acts 11:23), are encouraged to continue in grace (Acts 13:43), and are called to testify to the grace of God (Acts 20:24). Jesus says, "As the Father has sent me, even so, I am sending you" (John 20:21). God's mission is to the entire world.

·Our Future

God, and his grace, is everlasting. "Set your hope fully on the grace that will be brought to you at the revelation of Jesus Christ." (1 Peter 1:13)

·Our Hope Beyond Death

"Grace [reigns] through righteousness leading to eternal life through Jesus Christ our Lord." (Romans 5:21)

TABLE OF CONTENTS

INTRODUCTION

7 Deep Ministries — 14
Preface — 15

I. THE ROLES OF GOD

God of Peace — 19
God of Hope — 23
God of Love — 27
God is Love — 31

II. GOD'S GIFTS

God's Grace — 37
The Grace Graph — 39
God's Mercy — 41
The Mercy Graph — 43

III. UNDERSTANDING THE HOLY SPIRIT

Roles of Holy Spirit — 49

IV. THE FRUIT OF THE SPIRIT

Love	56
Joy	59
Patience	62
Kindness	67
Goodness	71
Faithfulness	78
Gentleness	83
Self-Control	87

V. CONCLUSION

Commitment	92
Prayer	95

CRYSTALYN MASON
Founder

Welcome to the Journey!

I'm Crystalyn Mason, and The Grace Gift sets a foundation to help build your identity in Christ Jesus! My workbook is loaded with questions and scriptures to help you find your identity in the Word of God. Negative experiences can bring forth fear in life, but when you know God is the most trustworthy person to rely on, you will see no need to fear.

I remember making the statement, "I don't need anyone, and I know what I'm doing" Then, as soon as I said it, God reminded me that apart from Him, I could do Nothing, but with Him, I could do everything. The grace gift helps you to understand who you are and whom you need. We need God, and we must hide in him.

Let's do the work together.

7 DEEP MINISTRIES

7DEEPMINISTRIESINTL@GMAIL.COM

7 DEEP MINISTRIES

In 2018 I regained my identity in Christ Jesus and thereafter my ministry, (7) Deep was established. Seven is the number of completion and deep is in reference to the Holy Spirit. I have experienced the Holy Spirit without limits. He has given me an understanding of salvation, inner healing, and progression as a Christian!

Did you know that 4 in 5 women have low self-esteem and nearly 75% of girls with low self-esteem admitted to engaging in self-destructive behaviors? I was 1 of those 4 in 5 women. The driving force of low self-esteem in my life was the need to feel accepted and approved. I'll share with you an excerpt from a book I am currently writing, "From The Bar Room to The Prayer Room," Here's my full testimony:
- When you're thirsty-pray.
- When you're hungry- read
- and both are required to be filled.

My life hasn't always been filled with prayer and the word of God. At the age of sixteen, I found myself at the bottom of a pit my parents divorced, and high school was a continuous cycle of self-destruction. I was trying to fill the void of approval and acceptance with alcohol, sex, and drugs. Join our private Facebook forum for open discussions and encouragement.

PREFACE

My power is strongest when you are weak." So, if Christ keeps giving me his power, I will gladly brag about how weak I am.
2 Corinthians 12:9

It is both humbling and exhilarating to receive something worth knowing you didn't pay for it. The truth is, when we receive God's grace, we have received a gift we didn't purchase. Grace is the free and undeserved gift that God gives as we respond to the call to become children of God.

"The Grace Gift" is personal for me because God's grace arrested me when I was still in the world searching for the things of this world. I played church, trying to find validation in others and fill voids that only grace could fill. God said, "Do you want to lose everything?" His voice was so clear that the only thing I could do was surrender! God opened my blind eyes, and I realized that my life was much more than I ever could consider it to be. God showed me through His Grace whose I was, who I am, and where I belong.

The Holy Spirit spoke to me, and I knew my Spirit, soul, and body had to change without compromise. I, at this point, chose to engulf myself in God's Word, praying, praising, and worshipping Him in Spirit, and in truth, God revealed my identity to show me that I was not a lost cause and there was still hope for me as long as I trusted in Him. God's Grace Gift opened my eyes to His unconditional love, joy, and other attributes of His character.

I now have the privilege of sharing His Grace Gift, salvation with others. This is how and why God has given me the mandate to draw souls closer to Him. God gave me specific instructions to enlighten the eyes of understanding in others. God reveals significant attributes of his nature. Within these pages, we use "OF and IS" quite a bit in relation to descriptions, functions of God, and the very identity of God. This book explores the gift in our lives and why He is so important to receive.

Section One

Understanding The Roles Of God

When we use the term "OF" in this section, it concerns the descriptions, functions, and roles of God.

God of Peace

Jehovah Shalom
Now may the God of peace Himself sanctify you completely; and may your whole spirit, soul, and body be preserved blameless at the coming of our Lord Jesus Christ. 1 Thessalonians 5:23

God is the source of peace – "For God is not the author of confusion but of peace, as in all the churches of the saints." 1 Corinthians 14:33. God is in the details of life.

> **Points to Ponder**
>
> The God of peace is a deep part of God's character, to have the peace of God requires an act of salvation.

As sovereign, omniscient (all-knowing) God, he is not frenzied, reactive, or bewildered; nothing catches Him off-guard. Instead, He precisely and intentionally orchestrates every event, even maneuvering man's persistent immoral behavior and sinful exercise of free will, to fulfill His ultimate purpose and plan.

The Process

> "
> I know what it's like to attempt to find peace in things of this world rather than finding peace in the One who provid*es* whole peace.
> "

Fill in the blank

In the past I have reached for _____ to give me peace.

Knowing what you know now about absolute peace, name three things the peace of God can bring you.

....

....

....

....

THE GRACE GIFT

NOTES

THE GRACE GIFT

NOTES

God of Hope

Miqweh Yisrael
Now may the God of hope fill you with all joy and peace in believing, that you may abound in hope by the power of the Holy Spirit. Romans 15:13

God is the source of hope, He is our plan for the future and he gives us hope to believe in Him. (Jeremiah 29:11) Hope is walking by faith and not by sight (2 Corinthians 5:7) and it is putting an expectation on the Holy Spirit for a move of God in life.

> **Points to Ponder**
>
> When the God of Hope begins to fill you with Joy and Peace, God is filling you with the fruits of His Spirit.
> (See Galatians 5:22)

When I hope in God, I place all of my trust in Him. Hope is trust that is expressed in our actions.

The Process

> I searched for hope and all I found was despair because I was looking for what I wanted. I was expecting what I wanted to come to pass instead of putting my hope in the hands who knew the plans He had for me.

Fill in the blank

How can you change what our flesh wants and place your hope in the hands of the Holy Spirit who knows you from the inside out.

....

....

....

....

....

NOTES

THE GRACE GIFT

NOTES

God of Love

Agape
For I am persuaded that neither death nor life, nor angels nor principalities, nor powers, nor things present nor things to come, not height nor depth, nor any other created thing shall be able to separate us from the love of God. Which is in Christ Jesus our LORD. Romans 8:38-39

Love is more than an emotion. It is a function referring to how someone operates. Our God of love felt so deeply about us that He sent his only begotten son. (John 3:16-17) Jesus came into the world and through His love. He took the keys away from death for you and me.

Points to Ponder

When we have accepted Jesus Christ in our lives. Nothing can separate us from the Love of God, physically or spiritually!

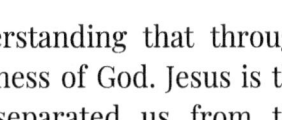

The Love of God gives the understanding that through Jesus Christ, we are the righteousness of God. Jesus is the purity that sets us apart. Sin separated us from the relationship and fellowship we could have with God. Then Jesus came and restored us to the father.

The Process

> *When I needed my soul to be loved and wanted the love that most of us want in fairy tales, God gave me someone to love me.*

Fill in the blank

I'm looking for the love of_____.

God wants you to look into the eyes of His love. Name some areas that God spoke to you from the verses above that can't separate you from His love.

_____

_____

_____

_____

_____

So, let's breakdown Romans 8:38-39
Nothing separates us from the love of God

- **Death nor life:**

The meaning is that when life ends physically, we pass away from this earth. The beginning of life is when we are born into this world. God wants us to know that nothing separates us from his love.

- **Angels nor principalities:**

Heavenly beings are the angels that God sends to us. Demons are the powers and principalities. God wants us to know that nothing separates us from his love.

- **Powers nor things present, nor things to come:**

Powers in the earth representing authority, the present things which are now, and the things to come still can't separate us from the love of God.

- **Height nor depth, nor any other created thing:**

Height is going to the heavens. Depths being the realm of Hell, can separate us from the love of God.

NOTES

God is Love

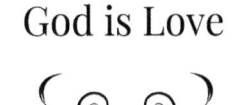

Agape

For I am persuaded that neither death nor life, nor angels nor principalities, nor powers, nor things present nor things to come, not height nor depth, nor any other created thing shall be able to separate us from the love of God. Which is in Christ Jesus our LORD. Romans 8:38-39

God has identified himself through Jesus, and we are seated in Christ Jesus, so we are united in promise.

> **Points to Ponder**
>
> God's love in action is when we confess our sins because we believe and know what Jesus did as the Son of God for the Son of man.

Do you hear Jesus? You hear that God is love. God sent Jesus to be the life, the truth, and the way to our eternal home in Heaven. (John 14:6) Jesus died for all; God did not place a title on a specific group. When He sent Jesus to represent unconditional love, He had you in mind the entire time. You are His because of who He is! LOVE!

The Process

> I was the person asking the same questions you are asking now. What is love? Where can I find Love? Is love even real? Is love painful? Like you, I experienced rejection thinking that I always had to have a "back up" so I wouldn't be left without love.

God says you are His because of who He is

Write a declaration stating that you are God's and express how it feels to be accepted by our creator.

_____

_____

_____

_____

_____

_____

NOTES

NOTES

Section Two

Understanding God's Gifts

For by grace, you have been saved through faith, and that not of yourselves; it is the gift of God, not of works, lest anyone should boast. Ephesian 2:8-9

Introduction

In this section, we will discuss the gifts of God. Jesus carries two of the richest and sweetest gifts I know, which are grace and mercy. Grace is receiving something that we don't deserve. For example, God sent His "ONLY" begotten Son that whosoever "BELIEVED" in Him would not perish but have everlasting life. I keep reiterating this throughout my book because understanding what Jesus did on the cross gives understanding to grace.

God was so moved with compassion for his children that He wanted to restore relationship and fellowship with him. Jesus carried a gift that many never understood until the fulfillment of God's plan and purpose. What was that gift? The gift of salvation. It can't be purchased or earned, yet it is knocking at the door of many hearts. When we were yet sinners, Christ still died for us.

God, the function of compassion, moved with the symbol or representation that mercy is given through an ultimate sacrifice for the world's sins. Let's shed light on the gifts of God that help us to understand the role of the Holy Spirit within us too...

God's Grace

> Let us, therefore, come boldly to the throne of Grace, that we may obtain mercy and find grace to help in time of need. Hebrews 4:16

I don't deserve the gifts God has given me. I am beginning to understand more and more about His unmerited grace. It cannot be measured and has no limitations. I will never understand this unconditional love living in grace. The more I learn about God, the more I want His grace. The ocean of grace is what we are drowning in, and grace lives in the air we breathe. Grace is God opening doors and closing doors that no man can open or shut. (See Revelation 3:8)

Grace is utterly amazing; it is greater than ALL of our sins. Grace lives in the blood of Jesus Christ; it is the favor of God. Our prayer should always be Lord. I never want to take your grace for granted.

The fact that we haven't died in our sin right on the spot is an ocean of grace given by God.

Grace can't be replaced with anything this world has to offer. Jesus is our saving grace, and the Holy Spirit is our changing grace. The strength to change and the ability to go through the process of change is in His Grace! Grace is deeper than all of these things; things the world has to offer are temporary, where grace is permanent, once accepted by faith! The depth of grace goes deeper than favor; it is a depth of unconditional love that saves our spirit, soul, and body.

Grace makes salvation available. It gives us the faith we need to believe what Jesus did for us. We obtain grace through faith! The gift of grace is given to us by God so no one can use pride to say, "I saved myself" or "Look at what I did." When you believe Jesus died on the cross for your sins, you have now entered salvation!

Table Review of God's Grace

Holy Spirit

- Love
- Joy
- Peace
- Patience
- Kindness
- Goodness
- Faithfulness

- Peace
- Rest
- Applied Wisdom
- Understanding
- Counsel
- Strength
- Knowledge
- Fear Of The Lord

Truth of God

Breathe of God

The Gift of Grace

NOTES

THE GRACE GIFT

God's Mercy

And when Jesus went out, He saw a great multitude; and He was moved with compassion for them and healed their sick. Matthew 14:14

In Matthew Chapter 14, Jesus' cousin, John the Baptist, was beheaded. Jesus departed to be by himself. Imagine the emotions Jesus felt during this loss? He lost a loved one, and more than that, he lost the one man who paved the road for His ministry. When we step into Jesus' shoes, I am sure he felt grief, and when you are grieving, you do not feel like being around anyone, much less a great multitude. So, what does it mean He was moved with compassion for them and healed their sick? He was not actually moving with his feet physically; He was moved within himself spiritually. He lost a loved one, yet compassion filled His heart. He saw the need to heal and give back to friends and families rather than focus on His grief. God's grace moved and motived mercy to bring a need. As you continue the story, you see where mercy moves again with the feeding of the five thousand.

Mercy releases a miracle,
becomes the answer to a prayer,
and releases through forgiveness.

In Matthew 18:27, we see a servant who owes the master a great deal of money, so the servant begs for more time to pay off the debt. Then the master of that servant was moved with compassion, released him, and forgave him the debt. The master granted the servant released from his obligations. Also, in chapter 18, you will see where Peter asks how many times should forgiveness be granted.

There is a key to mercy and forgiveness. Salvation through Jesus Christ is the key. God forgives us more times than we can count. We owe our lives to Him because Jesus paid the ultimate price on the cross of Calvary! He could have easily called angels to save Him from death; however, mercy moved Him, knowing how much God loved us. (See Matthew 26:53)

How does God love us like this?

nor do we understand God's, unconditional love. We live in a day and age where you have to meet a certain standard just to be loved like you are worth something. Matthew 18:27 gives us a parable of a servant that represents us and how we owe a debt that we cannot pay. The master represents Jesus, who was moved with mercy and became the sacrifice for the sin we could not pay! When we ask for forgiveness with a humble heart we are released from our sins. God's unconditional love is a standard set that you begin to understand through salvation.

> Did you know Jesus had to forgive us before He could be released into the arms of the Father? (See Luke 23:34,43)

Forgiveness releases you, not the other person. Now it does not excuse the other person for the choices they made. All you can do is continue to be a living example to those who don't know Jesus and need the same grace and mercy as you did. We are not excused from our sins and yet Jesus died on a cross to excuse them for us! Our choices put Him in a place where it should have been ours. Praise be to the God of our Savior when Grace sent mercy! See diagram on following page

Table Review of God's Mercy

Word Of God

- God's Changing Grace
- Transformation Process
- Romans 12:2

Anointing

- God's Saving Grace
- Salvation
- Ephesians 2:8

Jesus Christ

- God's Glorious Grace
- Reflection/Image
- 2 Corinthians 3:18

The Gift of Grace

NOTES

Review

- ·Jesus was sent by God to save the world from sin and death. (See John 3:16-17)

- Jesus died on the cross so we could be forgiven of our sin. (Matthew 27:45-66)

- Jesus paid a price we can never repay. (See 1 Peter 2:24-25)

- Jesus conquered death, we must confess our sin and believing in our hearts that he did this for us.
(See 1 John 1:9, 1 Corinthians 15:3-8,55-57)

Key Tips

- You're special to God
- Your sins are forgiven
- You can't repay God
- You are loved
- You're in His thoughts

Section Three

Understanding Our Holy Spirit

·But the Advocate, the Holy Spirit, whom the Father will send in my name, will teach you all things and will remind you of everything I have said to you. John 14:26

Role Of Holy Spirit

Who is the Holy Spirit, and how do we recognize Him?
We recognize Him by the truth God gives. God is Spirit, and He is truth. He has a holy personality. (See John 1:14, 4:24, 14:17)

*Holy means divine, heavenly, or superb. There is no one else like our God. *Spirit means to breathe. God is the breathe of truth. When we put His divine nature with His living word, we get a personality that is complete, whole, and full of life. (See Hebrews 4:12) Following are scriptures and verses that show you who the Holy Spirit of God is.

- John 1:32 And John bore witness, saying, "I saw the Spirit descending from Heaven like a dove, and He remained upon Him." When we see a dove, we tend to see a bird on the surface; in-depth, a dove represents love, commitment, and purity, a peace that only God can give. Why did the Spirit remain upon Jesus?

- When the Holy Spirit fell upon Jesus, He then became Jesus Christ, the Word of God, the anointing of God through the Spirit. Jesus Christ was now the fullness of God. (See Colossians 1:19-20, John 1:1, Acts 10:38)

So how does the Holy Spirit live in me once I accept Jesus Christ as my Savior?

As discussed, the Holy Spirit of God holds, has, and carries a personality. His personality includes rest, wisdom, understanding, counsel, might, knowledge, and fear of the Lord. When you count all of God's spiritual attributes of personalities, it equals seven. Seven is the number of perfection or completion. God allowed His completeness to be within and upon Jesus to make Him the Christ. God gives us insight and revelations of Him when we desire to experience him. In the experience, his personality becomes ours. It is important for us to always ask for more of Him. So, when you accept Jesus, you are also accepting God as your father and the Holy Spirit as your Comforter (see John 14:26). God sees you through Jesus. (See Galatians 2:20)

For example,

> Dear Lord, help me understand why your strength is so important versus my own. Help me apply your strength, so I bring you glory and honor in all that I do.
> In Jesus Name. Amen.

Review

- Who is the Helper? The Holy Spirit

- He draws you to Jesus (See John 6:44)

- ·He helps you when you are reading God's word (See Romans 12:2)

- He helps you when you pray (See Romans 8:26)

- Who sends the Holy Spirit? Father God

- Whose name does the Holy Spirit come in? The name of Jesus

Key Tips

- He offers friendship

- He offers truth

- He offers help

- He offers discernemnt

- He offers wisdom

THE GRACE GIFT

NOTES

Section Four

Understanding The Fruits of The Spirit

Fruit of the Spirit sums up nine attributes of a person living in accord with the Holy Spirit. Living in the fruit of the spirit means you are aware of the influence of the Holy Spirit.

HolySpirit Carries Love

Love is not a word to be thrown around or an action to be taken for granted. God demonstrates His love through a genuine sacrifice to love us while we were in the wrong. When Jesus said, "It is finished!" He claimed victory, the power over death and sin to give freedom and life. (See John 19:30)

Loving one another is knowing the love of God, his grace, and mercy. God loves us regardless of our status, situation, or shape; it's the same way we should love others. You have seen me toss in Romans 8:38-39 several times within this book; this verse turned my life around. I call this my life verse because I found my identity through the Word of God and His love. When I came to realize that this world could tear my body to shreds, fight me, or put me on a desert island to die like they did, John, I found shelter in the scripture that states nothing could separate me from God's love or His plan for my life. When life gets too chaotic, and people seek to take your life, please remember that the same applies to you; nothing can separate you from the love of God.

Love is a part of His Spirit. Please know that you may think you have time to get saved and know the love of God. The truth is, you don't have time to play on the fence. As the Holy Spirit draws you to the Lord, I pray that you won't ignore His love for you.

Review

- But God demonstrates His own love toward us in that while we were still sinners, Christ died for us. Romans 5:8

- Beloved, let us love one another for love is of God, and everyone who loves is born of God and knows God. 1 John 4:7

- For I am persuaded that neither death nor life, nor angels nor principalities nor powers, nor things present, nor things to come, nor height nor depth, nor any other created thing, shall be able to separate us from the love of God which is in Christ Jesus our LORD. Romans 8:38-39

Key Tips

He wants to meet your deepest needs

Love one another

Enjoy God's love

Nothing will sepaprate you two

Find safety in His love

THE GRACE GIFT

NOTES

Holy Spirit Carries Joy

You are not going to find contentment and joy in this world. We ask so many times why did Jesus find joy in the cross that was set before him, especially when the cross was a show of humiliation, torture, and public shame? Jesus found His delight in the cross because you were in mind. God asks us to walk by faith and not by sight, which includes believing that Jesus died for you even though you did not see Him physically die.

God wants you to experience Him through Jesus so you, too, can be filled with indescribable joy. We look for worldly things to supply us with joy many times. Food is good, shopping is good, too much of it begins to become an idol replacing supernatural joy with temporary happiness that isn't constant or fulfilling. (See Exodus 20:2) Seek God and want Him more than food, shopping, drugs, and alcohol; things like this are minute compared to the joy of being filled with righteousness, peace, and the Holy Spirit Himself.

> Do not rob yourself of this joy that God
> gives so freely through His grace and mercy!

Review

- Looking unto Jesus, the author and finisher of our faith, who for the joy that was set before Him endured the cross, despising the shame, and has sat down at the right hand of the throne of God. Hebrews 12:2

- Whom having not seen you love. Though now you do not see Him, yet believing, you rejoice with joy inexpressible and full of glory, receiving the end of your faith- the salvations of your souls. 1 Peter 1:8-9

- For the kingdom of God is not eating and drinking, but righteousness and peace and joy in the Holy Spirit. Romans 14:17

Key Tips

- Joy is set before you.
- You deserve joy
- Fix your heart on faith
- Be thankful
- You're chosen

NOTES

Holy Spirit Carries Patience

No one, including myself, likes their patience tested. We would rather have peace all the time, right? In the scriptures above, the writer of James says to count it "ALL JOY" when you "FALL" into various trials. Do you mean to tell me I must be joyful in trials? That is hard! Yes, You better believe it!

Why would our God of grace make us go through trials and ask us to count it all joy? God always has our best interest at heart. When our faith grows, our patience grows, and instead of taking things into our own hands, we can wait on God to move.

Patience is not a fruit of the Spirit to make us suffer. It is fruit to help us grow spiritually. We are not all-knowing like God, so we count it all joy that we are growing in God. The God of patience, which means both, comfort! Boy, that puts a fire in my step and rejoicing in my soul! The same God of grace and mercy is the God of patience and comfort.

God is patient with you, and he is the comfort
and help you need during your times of trials

Why is God so patient with me? Why does He want to comfort me?

When we are like-minded, that is unity; then we are also patient with one another. When we are patient, loving, and forgiving towards one another, we are representing Jesus Christ! There is so much power in unity, and knowing God is patient with me encourages me to know I can be patient with others and myself.

Be patient with yourself.

You and God make a united front. When you are in sync with God, he brings forth power through you that no one can stop, and that is powerful! Everyone grows at different rates, and you are a part of that everyone. You will grow with your relationship with God as you are patient with yourself through the process of progression. Grow in Christ, come off the milk and into the meat, and find your identity in Jesus! Patience is a powerful fruit.

Be willing to study the word of God and see just how patient He is with you. He wants no one to perish but to have everlasting life. See 2 Peter 3:9

Review

- ·My brethren count it all joy when you fall into various trials, knowing that the testing of your faith produces patience. James 1:2-3

- ·Now may the God of Patience and comfort grant you to be like minded toward one another, according to Christ Jesus. Romans 15:5

Key Tips

- See yourself as God does
- Be patient
- Don't stop growing
- He is patiently waiting for you
- Love is patient

THE GRACE GIFT

NOTES

NOTES

THE GRACE GIFT

Holy Spirit Carries Kindness

- What qualities of mind and character have you inherited?
- Where did you get those qualities?

The question is for self-evaluation. I say this because God's merciful kindness is great towards us, so we must learn to carry the same characteristic. Jesus was our example of the fruits of the Spirit of God; however, do we use Jesus' example to follow it? (See Matthew 7:12)

Remember mercy is moved with compassion, and where there is mercy, this is kindness. Kindness is useful. Kindness could plant a seed for someone who needs to know Jesus. When kindness is given with a move of compassion, love is the motive behind the motivation. When grace and mercy work together with the fruit of the Spirit, it's amazing to see it all transpire into one purpose, which is salvation. There is nothing we have done to deserve any of this.

Did you know God found you so valuable and worthy of so much love that Jesus did God's will of dying on the cross for you? This is God's merciful kindness that is so great towards us! Titus 3:5 states that not by righteousness or works we have done, but according to his mercy, he saved us. By the washing of regeneration and renewing of the Holy Spirit. I keep adding that there's nothing we did to deserve the gift from God. You may wonder what the scripture implies when it states the washing of regeneration and renewing of the Holy Spirit?

The meaning is,

When we are saved, our spirits are regenerated or brought back to life from sin. The Holy Spirit renews us completely, helping us to cultivate the fruits of the spirit. As a child of God through salvation, our desire to look like Jesus Christ should be an example to someone else who needs what we have. Our complete disposition, qualities of our mind and character, should look like Jesus. Kindness is not about us; it is about what we can give to others that will helpfully impact their lives.

Review

- For His merciful kindness is great towards us, and the truth of the Lord endures forever. Psalm 117:2

- But when the kindness and the love of God our savior toward man appeared, not by works of righteousness which we have done, but according to His mercy He saved us, through the washing of regeneration and renewing of the Holy Spirit. Titus 3:4,5

Key Tips

☐ Sacrifice today

☐ Impact a Life

☐ Fear God

☐ Be Kind and Gentle

☐ Give your troubles to God

NOTES

HolySpirit Carries Goodness

God created us in His image. (See Genesis 1:27) Jesus was able to use all five senses through His life, and it tells us how in these few passages of scripture. I want to show you how God uses His goodness through five senses to lead us to repentance that leads to change through salvation.

- The 1st sense is Taste.

Physically we use our mouths to taste whether something is good or bad. How do we taste God and know that He is good?
We can taste goodness through God's provision. God doesn't provide just food; He provides the air we breathe, the time we get to spend with family and friends, and He has provided His goodness through salvation! His grace is good, His mercy is good, and God is always good; there is no evil in Him. (See Mark 10:18) Goodness is healthy and happy; God's goodness spirit is so good that he sent Jesus. (See John 3:16)

- The 2nd sense is See

See that the Lord is good! Physically we see with our eyes, but God has given us spiritual eyes as well. God provides us with the ability to see the goodness of him through our spiritual eyesight. Do you see God's goodness?

Look at the cross. Do you see God's goodness there? When you look at the cross, do you see life or death?

It's a pretty deep question to ask, considering where your perspective is. If you only see death then
- You see Jesus dying as a human.
- You may see Him as the Pharisees saw Him, which is guilty.
- You may see Him as an ordinary man who dies on another cross.

It goes beyond the cross! If you see life, you see Jesus as one who came to give life and give it more abundantly. (See John 10:10)
- You will see Him as hope, love, and sacrifice.
- You will see Him as extraordinary and who died for life, to bring life to our Spirit and soul!

See the goodness of God through the cross. Seeing through faith making the impossible possible to see the goodness of God physically and more spiritually. When we trust in Him, to taste and see his goodness, we are blessed and happy.

You are chosen, hand-picked, and touched with love by love! Salvation is the love language of being adopted in God's family. (See Ephesians 1:5) God does not make a fake you, and if He wanted something like that, he would have created us to function on batteries, with an on and off switch. God wants something real! He made you with real feelings and a real mind and gave us free will. How we choose to use that free will is our choice. If you notice, robots are pre-programmed, and we are predestined with purpose! (See Romans 8:29)

- The 3rd sense is Hear

God will reveal things to you through His word and in spirit and truth. Jesus said, "I am the way, the truth, and the life, no one comes to the Father except through me."

Did you know sin will keep us from hearing God?

Here is the kicker we not only need to hear God; we must respond to his voice. Hearing His voice and moving to the sound of His voice brings forth the manifestation of Heaven in our lives. John 14:6 says, Jesus answered, "I am the way and the truth and the life. No one comes to the Father except through me. What does that mean?

Well, let's put it in today's perspective: The way is a direction., We have a path to choose Heaven or Hell. The world will tell you that you don't need God right now, and you have time to get your life together without him.
I want you to know that when you feel alone and unsure of who you are, let God show you the way that he is with you. (See John 1:12) and that you are His through Jesus! (See Joshua 1:5) Jesus is calling you. Don't wait. He knows you by name! Jesus called Lazarus by name, out of the grave, and he is calling yours today! (See John 11:43)

The 4th sense is Smell

The aroma of God is like the sweet smell of an apple pie cooling on a window sill that you can smell a mile away. I mean just imagine a sweet fresh fragrance that lingers and awakens every part of you, 2 Corinthians 2:15 describes us as a fragrance of Christ to God among those who are being saved and among those who are perishing. The presence of God is beautiful and sweet.

The 5th sense is Touch

Generally speaking, we touch with our hands. Physically we can hold the hand of another, feel the soft petals of a rose, or hold our children as we rock them to sleep. It's a touch that brings satisfaction. The Holy Spirit is the touch that brings our dry bones to life! He's the one who holds our hand by guiding us in the decisions of life with peace. He's the touch of comfort when our prayers are tears seeking forgiveness through repentance. Grace is a touch that can't be replaced by fulfillment of this world. Did you know that God created you with His hands? Look at Genesis 1:26-27,2:8. We were first His idea, then His design, and we were formed into His image! You have a purpose here. He made you with His hands, the touch of His love, peace, patience, and all other fruits of his spirit to grace us, with the ability to activate them through salvation! What a gift. The touch within us brings us closer to our creator! It's a touch you can't deny when one touch from the one who thought of you, created you and formed you can change your life forever.

Review

- Oh, taste and see that the Lord is good; Blessed is the man who trusts in Him! Psalm 34:8

- Then he said, "The God of our fathers has chosen you that you should know His will, and see the Just One, and hear the voice of His mouth. Acts 22:14

- Or do you despise the riches of His goodness, forbearance, and longsuffering, not knowing that the goodness of God leads you to repentance? Romans 2:4

Key Tips

- Use your senses
- Listen to God
- Taste his goodness around you
- God's goodness is rich
- Believe again

NOTES

NOTES

Holy Spirit Carries Faithfulness

The fruit of faithfulness, in two words, would be loyal and true. As we look at the three verses given, here is one thought to keep in mind,

- God is faithful, and his faithfulness is consistent. We can rely on Him, but we often fail when it comes to him relying on us.

More often than not, we do not want to admit when we have done wrong, especially unto God. God is Spirit, and though you can't see Him physically, He is omnipresent, which means He is everywhere. When you think no one else sees what you have done or what you are doing, God does. He is not blind to our hurts, needs, or difficulties, and He is not deaf to our cries. Confession is huge, and here is another little nugget for you that I adore about our heavenly Father. When you have no one else to talk to you, guess whom you can turn to? Yes! God himself will talk to you and with you. He doesn't want you to talk with Him and then put Him on the back burner until you need Him again. He is not a genie in a magic lamp, and he is not someone you take for granted. He wants to cultivate a relationship with you! God is faithful and just to forgive us when we confess our sins to Him. He wants us to talk to him about our fears, hopes, dreams, cares, worries and the above. He is just and what that means is He is a righteous God.

If you want to go a little deeper with just how "Just" He is look into Hebrews 6:17-18. He is a fair, precise, and exact God. He is not a God that he should lie because He is full of truth.

> *Our Senior Pastor Bud Womack said,*
> *"Confession is like throat punching the enemy."*

God is so faithful and just to forgive us of our sins, that when we confess our sins, Satan can no longer hold our mistakes over our heads!" Can I get an AMEN!? Why allow Satan to continue to hold your past over your head, when through salvation, by the blood of Jesus Christ, and using our mouths to confess those sins, the enemy is under our feet! (See Mark 16:15-18). God is faithful and just to forgive us from our unrighteousness when we confess them, we are using the authority God.

Review

- If we confess our sins, He is faithful and just to forgive us our sins and to cleanse us from all unrighteousness. 1 John 1:9

- God is faithful, by whom you were called into the fellowship of His Son, Jesus Christ our Lord. 1 Corinthians 1:9

- Then He who sat on the throne said, "Behold I make all things new." And He said to me, "write, for these words are true and faithful." Revelation 21:5

Key Tips

- God is faithful
- Be loyal to God
- If you make a mistake, repent!
- Live by faith
- Focus on what's true

NOTES

THE GRACE GIFT

NOTES

HolySpirit Carries Gentleness

Gentleness is the quality of being kind. If you know about the difference in quality and quantity, you will know that how you give gentleness outweighs the times you give it.

Here is an example,
 You may open a door for someone ten times a day. Still, you're showing your gentleness through your kindness. Let's say you see someone who could use a hot meal, so you serve the meal. Instead of walking away with a God bless you, you stay and talk with them, leading them to Jesus. Quality is the value of the time you put into something, where the quantity of kindness is the value of how many times you can do or be gentle.

Jesus said to take His yoke because He is gentle and lowly in heart. In Him, you will find rest. Jesus says this because the value of His gentleness is top-notch. You cannot put a price on the value of His Spirit of gentleness. He will spend all the time you want with Him; He will not push you away! It is salvation that is a shield of faith. It is the best of truth, and it is the love God gives you through His Son Jesus. (See Ephesians 6:14-20) He holds you up the way no one else can! All the fruits of the Spirit do not speak of the fruits in a way that is deceitful or in a way that chooses who receives them and who does not.

Review

·Take my yoke upon you and learn from me, for I am gentle and lowly in heart, and you will find rest for you souls. Matthew 11:29

·You have also given me the shield of your salvation; your right hand has held me up, your gentleness has made me great. Psalm 18:35

·But the wisdom that is from above is first pure, then peaceable, gentle, willing to yield, full of mercy and good fruits, without partiality and without hypocrisy. James 3:17

Key Tips

- Wisdom is peace and pure
- Be humble
- Quality is not Quantity
- Listen to understand

NOTES

NOTES

Holy Spirit Carries Self Control

Self Control is the ability to regulate one's emotions, thoughts, and behavior in the face of temptations and impulses. We have to exert control over our own thoughts, emotions, impulses, and performance. Self-control involves overriding or inhibiting something that would otherwise occur. Somehow, we ignore self-control, and I think we do because it requires true discipline and reliance on the Holy Spirit. The truth is self-control doesn't happen overnight. We must learn to adhere to new habits instead of the old habits we created. True power is submitting our flesh to Christ and walking in the Holy Spirit. We need to build upon our faith daily to know and understand how to apply self-control.

- Add to your faith virtue, virtue being pure and blameless, having an upright and clean heart.

- Add to your virtue knowledge, understanding what God has given you to apply it to your faith.

- Add to your knowledge self-control. You must know what God has given you, so you know how to apply it in your life.

People who lack self-control often give in to impulsive behavior and emotions. This means they may make poor choices that harm themselves or others .

Self-Control begins with love, and love covers a multitude of sins. Love washes away the past; as far as the east is from the west is in Jesus Christ! (See Psalm 103:1) The greatest example of self-control is Jesus. He was diligent, virtuous, with all knowledge of God. During temptations and emotions, He was Godly. He was a brother of kindness and still is. He showed the love of God by dying on the cross for us. (See Ephesians 1:17, 3:18-19, 1 John 4:9-10) Our self-control should look like the Spirit of God.

Review

- These three verses are a lot to take in, this is a fruit where we follow the Spirit and not our flesh where we listen to what the Spirit of the Lord is saying, hearing His will versus ours. (See Galatians 5:17, Luke 22:42)

Key Tips

- It's easy with God
- You're an overcomer
- Hear his will
- Follow the Spirit of God

NOTES

NOTES

Commitment

I, _____ (insert Name) receive and declare that I will Arise.
The blood of Jesus Christ saves me, and I am transformed by God's grace, mercy, and love. I am progressing on my journey with Jesus knowing that I am precious, bold, unique, and chosen by my heavenly Father. I understand that this challenge is just that, to challenge my heart, motives, strengths, and weaknesses.

I am committed to this challenge as I learn more about my Identity in Christ Jesus by leading the Holy Spirit.
I understand that my faith will be challenged within this process of learning God's plan, purpose, and promise for my life as He has called me to be whom He has created me to be. God says that I am made in the image of Jesus Christ. I am His, and He is mine. I decree and declare I can do this. I will do this because the relationship I have with Jesus means that much to me.

In Jesus Name. Amen.

Signed _____

Date:_____

NOTES

NOTES

Prayer

Dear Heavenly Father in the name of Jesus,
I confess to you that I am a sinner.
I believe in my heart that your Son, Jesus, came and died on the cross for my sins. Your word says that when I confess my sins (name them as the Holy Spirit leads) that you are faithful to forgive me. I believe Jesus rose again on the third day as your word says in Luke 24:46.

From this day forward I am yours. Thank you, Jesus for saving my life. I love you and guide me to find my identity in you and to be more like you.
In Jesus Name.
Amen.

Welcome to the family!
Welcome to Love, Hope, Peace, and Joy!
Welcome to Life!
Let the heavens rejoice as they, and I, welcome you home!

NOTES

NOTES

NOTES

Thank you
for reading

As you have read and studied through The Grace Gift, it is my prayer that the Holy Spirit has revealed to you how genuinely loved and valued you are. I want to lead you through a prayer of confession for salvation in your life. Remember to pray out loud (see John 1:9) let this prayer be a guidance prayer for you. Come back to it often. Keep a repentant heart.

THE CHRISTIAN PUBLISHING COMPANY

CONTACT US TODAY

WEBSITE: LIVINGWATERBOOKS.ORG

www.ingramcontent.com/pod-product-compliance
Lightning Source LLC
Chambersburg PA
CBHW070314100426
42743CB00011B/2446